interchange

FIFTH EDITION

1A

Workbook

Jack C. Richards

with Jonathan Hull and Susan Proctor

CAMBRIDGE
UNIVERSITY PRESS

CAMBRIDGE
UNIVERSITY PRESS

University Printing House, Cambridge CB2 8BS, United Kingdom

One Liberty Plaza, 20th Floor, New York, NY 10006, USA

477 Williamstown Road, Port Melbourne, VIC 3207, Australia

314–321, 3rd Floor, Plot 3, Splendor Forum, Jasola District Centre, New Delhi – 110025, India

103 Penang Road, #05-06/07, Visioncrest Commercial, Singapore 238467

Cambridge University Press is part of the University of Cambridge.

It furthers the University's mission by disseminating knowledge in the pursuit of education, learning and research at the highest international levels of excellence.

www.cambridge.org
Information on this title: www.cambridge.org/9781316622544

© Cambridge University Press 1990, 2017

First published 1990
Second edition 1997
Third edition 2005
Fourth edition 2013
Fifth edition 2017
Fifth edition update published 2021

20 19 18 17 16 15 14 13 12 11 10 9

Printed in Great Britain by CPI Group (UK) Ltd, Croydon CR0 4YY

A catalogue record for this publication is available from the British Library.

ISBN 978-1-009-04044-0 Student's Book 1 with eBook
ISBN 978-1-009-04047-1 Student's Book 1A with eBook
ISBN 978-1-009-04048-8 Student's Book 1B with eBook
ISBN 978-1-009-04063-1 Student's Book 1 with Digital Pack
ISBN 978-1-009-04064-8 Student's Book 1A with Digital Pack
ISBN 978-1-009-04065-5 Student's Book 1B with Digital Pack
ISBN 978-1-316-62247-6 Workbook 1
ISBN 978-1-316-62254-4 Workbook 1A
ISBN 978-1-316-62266-7 Workbook 1B
ISBN 978-1-108-40606-2 Teacher's Edition 1
ISBN 978-1-316-62226-1 Class Audio 1
ISBN 978-1-009-04066-2 Full Contact 1 with Digital Pack
ISBN 978-1-009-04067-9 Full Contact 1A with Digital Pack
ISBN 978-1-009-04068-6 Full Contact 1B with Digital Pack
ISBN 978-1-108-40306-1 Presentation Plus 1

Additional resources for this publication at cambridgeone.org

Contents

Credits

Illustrations

Pablo Gallego (Beehive Illustration): 42, 53, 65, 78, 91; **Thomas Girard** (Good Illustration): 3, 25, 50, 72, 92; **Quino Marin** (The Organisation): 2, 47, 54, 66; **Gavin Reece** (New Division): 15, 48, 52(B); **Paul Williams** (Sylvie Poggio Artists): 51.

Photos

Back cover (woman with whiteboard): Jenny Acheson/Stockbyte/GettyImages; Back cover (whiteboard): Nemida/GettyImages; Back cover (man using phone): Betsie Van Der Meer/Taxi/GettyImages; Back cover (woman smiling): PeopleImages.com/DigitalVision/GettyImages; Back cover (name tag): Tetra Images/GettyImages; Back cover (handshake): David Lees/Taxi/GettyImages; p. 1: Jon Feingersh/Blend Images/Brand X Pictures/GettyImages; p. 4 (TL): Juanmonino/iStock/GettyImages Plus/GettyImages; p. 4 (BL): Caiaimage/Chris Ryan/OJO+/GettyImages; p. 4 (TR): XiXinXing/GettyImages; p. 4 (BR): powerofforever/E+/GettyImages; p. 5: PeopleImages/DigitalVision/GettyImages; p. 6: Martin Barraud/Caiaimage/GettyImages; p. 7 (photo 1): Jetta Productions/Blend Images/GettyImages; p. 7 (photo 2): Oleksandr Rupeta/NurPhoto/GettyImages; p. 7 (photo 3): Hill Street Studios/Blend Images/GettyImages; p. 7 (photo 4): Jupiterimages/Photolibrary/GettyImages; p. 8: Monty Rakusen/Cultura/GettyImages; p. 9: Matt Hage/Design Pics/First Light/GettyImages; p. 10 (TL): Digital Vision/DigitalVision/GettyImages; p. 10 (TR): Hybrid Images/Cultura/GettyImages; p. 10 (BR): kali9/E+/GettyImages; p. 11: kali9/E+/GettyImages; p. 12 (T): Hybrid Images/Cultura/GettyImages; p. 12 (BL): Visage/Stockbyte/GettyImages; p. 12 (BC): segawa7/iStock/GettyImages Plus/GettyImages; p. 12 (BR): asterix0597/E+/GettyImages; p. 13: Westend61/GettyImages; p. 14: Robert Niedring/Alloy/GettyImages; p. 16 (silver earrings): JohnGollop/iStock/GettyImages Plus/GettyImages; p. 16 (gold earrings): cobalt/iStock/GettyImages Plus/GettyImages; p. 16 (leather coat): bonetta/iStock/GettyImages Plus/GettyImages; p. 16 (wool coat): DonNichols/E+/GettyImages; p. 16 (orange shirt): rolleiflextlr/iStock/GettyImages Plus/GettyImages; p. 16 (gray shirt): popovaphoto/iStock/GettyImages Plus/GettyImages; p. 16 (cotton dresses): Evgenii Karamyshev/Hemera/GettyImages Plus/GettyImages; p. 16 (silk dresses): Paolo_Toffanin/iStock/GettyImages Plus/GettyImages; p. 17 (gold ring): Image Source/GettyImages; p. 17 (silver ring): ProArtWork/E+/GettyImages; p. 17 (tablet): luismmolina/E+/GettyImages; p. 17 (laptop computer): Howard Kingsnorth/The Image Bank/GettyImages; p. 17 (hiking boots): AlexRaths/iStock/GettyImages Plus/GettyImages; p. 17 (sneakers): badmanproduction/iStock/GettyImages Plus/GettyImages; p. 17 (wool gloves): popovaphoto/iStock/GettyImages Plus/GettyImages; p. 17 (leather gloves): Hugh Threlfall/Stockbyte/GettyImages; p. 17 (black sunglasses): Vladimir Liverts/Hemera/GettyImages Plus/GettyImages; p. 17 (white sunglasses): Dimedrol68/iStock/GettyImages Plus/GettyImages; p. 18 (photo 3): csfotoimages/iStock/GettyImages Plus/GettyImages; p. 18 (photo 1): Donald Iain Smith/Moment/GettyImages; p. 18 (photo 4): goir/iStock/GettyImages Plus/GettyImages; p. 18 (photo 2): Marc Romanelli/Blend Images/GettyImages; p. 19 (T): Larry Busacca/GettyImages Entertainment/GettyImages North America/GettyImages; p. 19 (B): Steve Granitz/WireImage/GettyImages; p. 20 (photo 1): Brian Bahr/GettyImages North America/GettyImages; p. 20 (photo 2): Phillip Faraone/GettyImages North America/GettyImages; p. 20 (photo 3): Anthony Harvey/GettyImages Entertainment/GettyImages Europe/GettyImages; p. 20 (photo 4): Taylor Hill/FilmMagic/GettyImages; p. 20 (BR): Jon Kopaloff/FilmMagic/GettyImages; p. 21 (R): DianaHirsch/E+/GettyImages; p. 21 (L): ILM/Universal Studios/GettyImages; p. 23 (T): Shirlaine Forrest/WireImage/GettyImages; p. 23 (B): Moof/Cultura/GettyImages; p. 24 (T): Mike Windle/GettyImages Entertainment/GettyImages North America/GettyImages; p. 24 (B): Donald Miralle/DigitalVision/GettyImages; p. 26: Copyright Anek/Moment/GettyImages; p. 27 (photo 1): Echo/Cultura/GettyImages; p. 27 (photo 2): Juice Images/Cultura/GettyImages; p. 27 (photo 3): Christopher Hope-Fitch/Moment/GettyImages; p. 27 (photo 4): sjenner13/iStock/GettyImages Plus/GettyImages; p. 27 (photo 5): Hero Images/GettyImages; p. 30 (L): Soumen Nath Photography/Moment Open/GettyImages; p. 30 (R): Chaos/The Image Bank/GettyImages; p. 31 (L): Tetra Images/GettyImages; p. 31 (R): John Freeman/Dorling Kindersley/GettyImages; p. 33 (T): Westend61/GettyImages; p. 33 (B): Adam Gault/Photodisc/GettyImages; p. 34 (T): Camilla Watson/AWL Images/GettyImages; p. 34 (C): Stephen McCarthy/Sportsfile/GettyImages; p. 34 (B): PhotoAlto/Laurence Mouton/PhotoAlto Agency RF Collections/GettyImages; p. 35: Koji Aoki/Aflo/GettyImages; p. 36: PeopleImages/DigitalVision/GettyImages; p. 37: Jan Speiser/EyeEm/GettyImages; p. 38 (L): PeopleImages/DigitalVision/GettyImages; p. 38 (R): asiseeit/E+/GettyImages; p. 40 (T): PRASIT CHANSAREEKORN/Moment/GettyImages; p. 40 (B): Tuul and Bruno Morandi/Photolibrary/GettyImages; p. 41 (T): Boy_Anupong/Moment/GettyImages; p. 41 (B): John W Banagan/Lonely Planet Images/GettyImages; p. 46 (L): Allison Michael Orenstein/The Image Bank/GettyImages; p. 46 (R): Plume Creative/DigitalVision/GettyImages; p. 49: Jim Franco/Taxi/GettyImages; p. 52 (boots): StockPhotosArt/iStock/GettyImages Plus/GettyImages; p. 52 (cap): ljpat/E+/GettyImages; p. 52 (dress): pidjoe/E+/GettyImages; p. 52 (high heels): LOVE_LIFE/iStock/GettyImages Plus/GettyImages; p. 52 (jeans): gofotograf/iStock/GettyImages Plus/GettyImages; p. 52 (jewelry): DEA/L. DOUGLAS/De Agostini Editorial/GettyImages; p. 52 (necktie): WilshireImages/E+/GettyImages; p. 52 (shirt): Alex Cao/Photodisc/GettyImages; p. 52 (shorts): stocksnapper/iStock/GettyImages Plus/GettyImages; p. 52 (sneakers): Tevarak/iStock/GettyImages Plus/GettyImages; p. 52 (suit): bonetta/iStock/GettyImages Plus/GettyImages; p. 52 (T-shirt): GaryAlvis/E+/GettyImages; p. 55 (T): Blake Little/Stone/GettyImages; p. 55 (C): Jenner Images/Moment Open/GettyImages; p. 55 (B): Kevin Kozicki/Image Source/GettyImages; p. 56: Barry Austin Photography/Iconica/GettyImages; p. 57 (photo 1): sutichak/iStock/GettyImages Plus/GettyImages; p. 57 (photo 2): Koichi Kamoshida/Photolibrary/GettyImages; p. 57 (photo 3): Westend61/GettyImages; p. 57 (photo 4): Paul Bradbury/OJO/GettyImages; p. 57 (photo 5): Jan Hetfleisch/GettyImages Europe/GettyImages; p. 57 (photo 6): Halfdark/GettyImages; p. 58 (T): Jupiterimages/Photos.com/GettyImages Plus/GettyImages; p. 58 (B): Nmaverick/iStock/GettyImages Plus/GettyImages; p. 59 (text messaging): skynesher/E+/GettyImages; p. 59 (rugby match): Stewart Cohen/Photolibrary/GettyImages; p. 59 (sushi): Steve Brown Photography/Photolibrary/GettyImages; p. 59 (houston): Gavin Hellier/Photographer's Choice/GettyImages; p. 60: Sam Edwards/Caiaimage/GettyImages; p. 61 (L): Martin Puddy/Stone/GettyImages; p. 61 (R): Karina Wang/Photographer's Choice/GettyImages; p. 62 (L): jimkruger/iStock/GettyImages Plus/GettyImages; p. 62 (C): AzmanL/iStock/GettyImages Plus/GettyImages; p. 62 (R): Jonas Gratzer/LightRocket/GettyImages; p. 63 (T): Alberto Manuel Urosa Toledano/Moment/GettyImages; p. 63 (B): DUCEPT Pascal/hemis.fr/GettyImages; p. 64 (BL): Sungjin Kim/Moment Open/GettyImages; p. 64 (TC): RODRIGO BUENDIA/AFP/GettyImages; p. 64 (BR): Andrea Pistolesi/Photolibrary/GettyImages; p. 65: JTB/UIG/GettyImages; p. 68: BSIP/UIG/GettyImages; p. 69: KidStock/Blend Images/GettyImages; p. 70: YinYang/E+/GettyImages; p. 71: Ariel Skelley/Blend Images/GettyImages; p. 73 (photo 1): Peter Dazeley/Photographer's Choice/GettyImages; p. 73 (photo 2): whitewish/E+/GettyImages; p. 73 (photo 3): Chuck Kahn/EyeEm/GettyImages; p. 73 (photo 4): lisafx/iStock/GettyImages Plus/GettyImages; p. 73 (photo 5): TUGIO MURATA/amanaimagesRF/GettyImages; p. 73 (photo 6): Creative Crop/DigitalVision/GettyImages; p. 74 (greasy): David Crunelle/EyeEm/GettyImages; p. 74 (bland): Howard Shooter/GettyImages; p. 74 (rich): Johner Images/GettyImages; p. 74 (salty): Creativ Studio Heinemann/GettyImages; p. 74 (healthy): Verdina Anna/Moment/GettyImages; p. 75 (Carlota): andresr/E+/GettyImages; p. 75 (Luka): NicolasMcComber/E+/GettyImages; p. 75 (Adam): David Harrigan/Canopy/GettyImages; p. 76 (broccoli): Kevin Summers/Photographer's Choice/GettyImages; p. 76 (sushi): Food Image Source/StockFood Creative/GettyImages; p. 76 (cream cone): dlerick/E+/GettyImages; p. 77: gchutka/E+/GettyImages; p. 79 (T): Richard Roscoe/Stocktrek Images/GettyImages; p. 79 (C): www.sierralara.com/Moment/GettyImages; p. 79 (B): Yevgen Timashov/Cultura/GettyImages; p. 80: Ulf Andersen/GettyImages Europe/GettyImages; p. 81 (Badwater Basin): David ToussaintMoment/GettyImages; p. 81 (Suez Canal): Jacques Marais/Gallo Images/GettyImages; p. 81 (Mount Waialeale): M Swiet Productions/Moment Open/GettyImages; p. 82: Christian Vorhofer/imageBROKER/GettyImages; p. 83 (Angel Falls): Jane Sweeney/AWL Images/GettyImages; p. 83 (Yangtze River): View Stock/GettyImages; p. 83 (Antarctica): Michael Nolan/robertharding/GettyImages; p. 83 (Rain forest): JohnnyLye/iStock/GettyImages Plus/GettyImages; p. 83 (Grand Canyon): Stephanie Hohmann/EyeEm/GettyImages; p. 84: GlobalP/iStock/GettyImages Plus/GettyImages; p. 86: Emilio Cobos/Euroleague Basketball/GettyImages; p. 87 (go to park): Feverpitched/iStock/GettyImages Plus/GettyImages; p. 87 (go to concerts): Yuri_Arcurs/DigitalVision/GettyImages; p. 87 (have parties): SolStock/E+/GettyImages; p. 87 (see plays): VisitBritain/Eric Nathan/Britain On View/GettyImages; p. 87 (watch horror movies): Crazytang/E+/GettyImages; p. 87 (go on picnics): Kentaroo Tryman/Maskot/GettyImages; p. 88 (Hannah): Dianne Avery Photography/GettyImages; p. 88 (Pablo): Jacqueline Veissid/Blend Images/GettyImages; p. 88 (Richard): Laura Doss/Image Source/GettyImages; p. 88 (Lien): iPandastudio/iStock/GettyImages Plus/GettyImages; p. 88 (Kalil): Juanmonino/E+/GettyImages; p. 88 (Rachel): Westend61/GettyImages; p. 88 (Eliana): billnoll/E+/GettyImages; p. 88 (Daichi): petekarici/iStock/GettyImages Plus/GettyImages; p. 90: ichaka/E+/GettyImages; p. 93 (L): Paul Bradbury/Caiaimage/GettyImages; p. 93 (TR): Hero Images/GettyImages; p. 93 (CR): Hero Images/DigitalVision/GettyImages; p. 94: Zero Creatives/Cultura/GettyImages; p. 95 (T): DragonImages/iStock/GettyImages Plus/GettyImages; p. 95 (C): agentry/iStock/GettyImages Plus/GettyImages; p. 95 (B): Digital Vision/Photodisc/GettyImages; p. 96: Deb Snelson/Moment/GettyImages.

1 Where are you from?

1 Write about yourself.

My first name is _____.

My last name is _____.

Please call me _____.

I'm from _____.

2 Put the words in order to make questions. Then answer the questions.

1. class   your   how   English   is

A: _How is your English class_ _____?

B: _It's pretty interesting_ _____.

2. name   teacher's   your   what's

A: _____?

B: _____.

3. from   your   teacher   where   is

A: _____?

B: _____.

4. your   what   friends'   are   names

A: _____?

B: _____.

5. classmates   what   your   are   like

A: _____?

B: _____.

3 Choose the correct responses.

1. A: Hi, I'm Diane.

   B: *Oh, hi. I'm Peter.*

     • Oh, hi. I'm Peter.

     • What do people call you?

2. A: My name is Bill Matory.

   B: _____

     • Nice to meet you, Bill.

     • Let's go and say hello.

3. A: Hello. I'm a new student here.

   B: _____

     • Thanks.

     • Welcome.

4. A: I'm sorry. What's your name again?

   B: _____

     • P-A-R-K.

     • Eun-ha Park.

5. A: How do you spell your first name?

   B: _____

     • I'm Akira.

     • A-K-I-R-A.

6. A: What do people call you?

   B: _____

     • It's Angela Young.

     • Everyone calls me Angie.

4 Look at the answers. What are the questions?

1. Agent: What *'s your name?* _____

   Silvia: My name's Silvia.

2. Agent: What _____

   Silvia: My last name's Garcia.

3. Agent: Who _____

   Silvia: That's my husband.

4. Agent: What _____

   Silvia: His name is Gustavo.

5. Agent: Where _____

   Silvia: We're from Venezuela.

6. Agent: Who _____

   Silvia: They're my children.

5 Choose the correct words.

1. That's Antonio. _____He_____ is in my class. (He / His)

2. I'm from Barcelona, Spain. _____ is a beautiful city. (It / It's)

3. Excuse me. What's _____ last name again? (you / your)

4. They're my classmates. _____ names are Jill and Tae-min. (They / Their)

5. _____ name is Naoko. Please call me Nao. (I / My)

6. This is Ellen's husband. _____ name is Tim. (His / Her)

7. My parents are on vacation. _____ are in Australia. (We / They)

8. We have English at 10:00. _____ classroom number is 108-C. (Our / We)

6 Complete this conversation with *am, are,* or *is.*

Amber: Who _____are_____ the men over there, Ethan?

Ethan: Oh, they _____ on my baseball team. Let me introduce you. Hi, Pablo, this _____ Amber Fox.

Pablo: Nice to meet you, Amber.

Amber: Nice to meet you, too. Where _____ you from?

Pablo: I _____ from Cuba.

Ethan: And this _____ Marco. He _____ from Brazil.

Lisa: Hi, Marco.

7 Hello and welcome!

A Read these four student biographies. Then complete the chart below.

⟫⟫⟫ INTERNATIONAL LANGUAGE SCHOOL ⟪⟪⟪

Every month, we meet new students at the school. This month, we want to introduce four new students to you. Please say "hello" to them!

Rafael is in English 101. He is from Puebla, Mexico. His first language is Spanish, and he also speaks a little French. He wants to be on the school volleyball team. He says he doesn't play very well, but he wants to learn!

Su-yin is in English 102. She is from Wuhan, China. She says she writes and reads English pretty well, but she needs a lot of practice speaking English. Her first language is Chinese. She wants to play volleyball on the school team.

Fatima is in English 103. She is from Tunis, Tunisia. She speaks Arabic and French. She is an engineering student. She wants to be an engineer. She says she doesn't play any sports. She wants to make a lot of new friends in her class.

Finally, meet **Arun**. He is in Fatima's class. He says he speaks English well, but his writing isn't very good! Arun is from Chennai, India, and his first language is Hindi. He is a soccer player, and he wants to be on the school soccer team.

Name	Where from	Languages	Sports
1. Rafael			
2.	Tunis, Tunisia		
3.		English and Chinese	
4.			soccer

B Write a short biography of a classmate.

_____

_____

_____

_____

_____

8 Choose the correct sentences to complete this conversation.

- ☐ You, too. Talk to you later.
- ☑ Hi, Stacey. I'm Omar. How are you?
- ☐ I really like biology.
- ☐ Yes, I am. I'm an exchange student from Egypt.
- ☐ Yes, he is. We're in Biology 300. Is he your friend?

Stacey: Hello, I'm Stacey.

Omar: _Hi, Stacey. I'm Omar. How are you?_

Stacey: Pretty good, thanks. Are you a student here?

Omar: _____

Stacey: Welcome. Do you like it here? What's your favorite subject?

Omar: _____

Stacey: Oh, really? Is Ben Jones in your class?

Omar: _____

Stacey: No, he's my brother! Actually, I have to go meet him now. Nice to meet you, Omar.

Omar: _____

9 Complete this conversation. Use contractions where possible.

> **Grammar note: Contractions**
>
> **Do not use contractions for short answers with Yes.**
>
> Are you from Argentina?   Is he from Greece?
>   Yes, I am. (*not* Yes, I'm.)   Yes, he is. (*not* Yes, he's.)

Alex: Hello. ___I'm___ Alex Robles.
And this is my sister Celia.

Paola: Hi. _____ Paola Vieira.

Celia: Are you from South America, Paola?

Paola: Yes, _____. _____ from Brazil.
Where are you both from?

Alex: _____ from Puerto Rico.

Paola: Are you from San Juan?

Celia: No, _____. _____ from
Ponce. By the way, are you in English
101?

Paola: No, _____. I'm in English 102.

10 Look at the answers. What are the questions?

1. **A:** _Who's Allison?_

   B: Allison is my best friend.

2. **A:** _____

   B: My favorite school subject is history.

3. **A:** _____

   B: No, we're not from Germany. We're from Switzerland.

4. **A:** _____

   B: Yes, it's an interesting class.

5. **A:** _____

   B: Yes, Mary and Yuka are in my class.

6. **A:** _____

   B: Ryan is funny and friendly.

7. **A:** _____

   B: No, Ms. Rogers isn't my English teacher. She's my math teacher.

11 Read the expressions. Which ones say "hello" and which ones say "good-bye"?

	Hello	Good-bye
1. How are you?	✓	☐
2. See you tomorrow.	☐	☐
3. Good night.	☐	☐
4. Good morning.	☐	☐
5. Talk to you later.	☐	☐
6. How's it going?	☐	☐
7. Have a good day.	☐	☐
8. What's up?	☐	☐

12 Answer these questions about yourself. Use contractions where possible.

1. Are you on vacation? _____

2. Is your teacher from Canada? _____

3. Is your first name popular? _____

4. Is your English class in the morning? _____

5. Are you from Asia? _____

6. Are you a student at a university? _____

2 What do you do?

1 **Match the correct words to make sentences.**

1. A cashier   _d_
2. A vendor   _____
3. A babysitter   _____
4. A doctor   _____
5. A tutor   _____
6. A pet sitter   _____

a. helps sick people.
b. takes care of animals.
c. sells things.
d. takes money and gives change.
e. takes care of children.
f. helps students with their school work.

2 **Write sentences using _He_ or _She_.**

1. I'm a mechanic. I fix cars. I work in a garage.
   He's a mechanic. He fixes cars.
   He works in a garage.

2. I'm a cook. I cook food. I work in a restaurant.
   She _____
   _____

3. I'm a math teacher. I teach math to students. I work in a school.
   She _____
   _____

4. I'm a taxi driver. I drive a car. I take people to places they want to go.
   _He_ _____
   _____

3 Write *a* or *an* in the correct places.

1. He's ⌄*a* carpenter. He works for ⌄*a* construction company. He builds schools and houses.

2. She's office manager. She works for large company. It's interesting job.

3. He works in restaurant. He's server. He's also part-time student. He takes business class in the evening.

4. She works for travel company. She arranges tours. She's travel agent.

5. He has difficult job. He's flight attendant. He works on airplane.

4 Choose someone in your family. Write about his or her job.

_____

_____

_____

_____

5 Complete this conversation with the correct words.

Tiffany: What _____does_____ your brother _____, exactly?
(do / does)   (do / does)

Kate: He _____ for the city. He's a firefighter.
(work / works)

Tiffany: How _____ he _____ it?
(do / does)   (like / likes)

Kate: It's an interesting job. He _____ it very much.
(like / likes)

But he _____ long hours. And what _____ you _____?
(work / works)   (do / does)   (do / does)

Tiffany: I'm a student. I _____ geography.
(study / studies)

Kate: Oh, really? Where _____ you _____ to school?
(do / does)   (go / goes)

Tiffany: I _____ to Matthews University. My brother _____ there, too.
(go / goes)   (go / goes)

Kate: Really? And what _____ he _____?
(do / does)   (study / studies)

Tiffany: He _____ graphic design.
(study / studies)

Kate: That sounds interesting.

6 Complete the questions in this conversation.

Tom: _Where do you work?_

Ray: I work for Brady Corporation.

Tom: And what _____
there?

Ray: I'm an accountant.

Tom: An accountant? How

_____

Ray: I like numbers, so it's a great job.
And what _____

Tom: I'm a teacher.

Ray: Really? What _____

Tom: I teach accounting!

7 Interesting jobs

Read these two interviews. Answer the questions.

Today, Job Talk interviews two people with interesting jobs.

Job Talk: Oliver, where do you work?

Oliver: Well, I guess I work in the sky.

Job Talk: In the sky? What do you do?

Oliver: I'm a flight attendant. I work on the international flight from Miami to Recife, Brazil.

Job Talk: That's really interesting. What do you like best about your job?

Oliver: I really like to travel and to meet people. So my job is perfect for me.

Job Talk: Do you speak Portuguese?

Oliver: I speak a little. I carry my dictionary everywhere I go!

Job Talk: What do you do, Lucy?

Lucy: I'm a security guard at Matthews University.

Job Talk: That sounds difficult. What is the hardest thing about your job?

Lucy: Well, people break the rules at the university, and I have to stop them.

Job Talk: Are people unfriendly to you?

Lucy: Sometimes, but most of the students are very nice.

Job Talk: And what do you like best about your job?

Lucy: Well, some days the university is quiet. I get to read a lot of books!

1. What does Oliver do?   He _____
2. Where does he work?   _____
3. How does Oliver learn Portuguese? _____
4. What does Lucy do?   She _____
5. Where does she work?   _____
6. What is the hardest part of her job? _____

8 Meet Patricio. Write questions about him using *What, Where, When,* and *How.*

1. _What does he do?_
2. _____
3. _____
4. _____

Mercy Hospital

Patricio Cardozo
Registered Nurse,
Night Shift

9 **How does Patricio spend his weekends? Complete this paragraph with the words from the box.**

☐ around	☐ at	☐ before	☐ early
☐ in	☐ late	☑ on	☐ until

Everyone knows Patricio at the hospital. Patricio is a part-time nurse. He works at night on weekends. _____On_____ Saturdays and Sundays, Patricio sleeps most of the day and wakes up a little _____ nine _____ the evening, usually at 8:45 or 8:50. He has breakfast very late, _____ 9:30 or 10:00 P.M.! He watches television _____ eleven o'clock and then starts work _____ midnight. _____ in the morning, usually around 5:00 A.M., he leaves work, has a little snack, goes home, goes to bed, and sleeps _____. It's a perfect schedule for Patricio. He's a pre-med student on weekdays at a local college.

10 **Choose the correct words to complete the sentences.**

1. Avery is a tour guide. She _____takes_____ (answers / takes / writes) people on tours.

2. Stella _____ (does / goes / starts) to bed after midnight.

3. Bonnie _____ (answers / gets / starts) up early in the morning.

4. What _____ (does / goes / serves) your sister do?

5. Roland _____ (answers / serves / starts) work at 8:00 A.M.

6. My brother works in a bookstore. He _____ (answers / sells / works) books and magazines.

7. The Havana Garden restaurant _____ (serves / takes / writes) good Cuban food.

8. Dan _____ (serves / does / works) his school work on his new computer.

9. Nunu _____ (goes / sells / writes) about 30 emails a day.

10. David is a receptionist. He _____ (answers / starts / types) the phone and greets people.

11. Miguel _____ (does / takes / works) in a restaurant.

11 Choose the sentences in the box that have the same meaning as the sentences below.

- [ ] He goes to the university.
- [ ] She cares for people's pets.
- [ ] She stays up late.
- [ ] What does he do?
- [x] She's a fitness instructor.
- [ ] He works part-time.

1. She teaches exercise classes.

She's a fitness instructor.

2. What's his job?

_____

3. She's a pet sitter.

_____

4. He's a student.

_____

5. She goes to bed at midnight.

_____

6. He works three hours every day.

_____

12 Fill in the missing words or phrases from these job advertisements.

1.
- [ ] at night
- [ ] part-time
- [x] servers
- [ ] weekends

2.
- [ ] interesting
- [ ] Japanese
- [ ] tours
- [ ] student

3.
- [ ] at
- [ ] in
- [ ] manager
- [ ] weekends

Help Wanted

Larry's Diner needs

_____servers_____. Work during

the day or _____,

weekdays or _____,

full-time or _____.

Call 901–555–1977.

_____ job for a

language _____.

Take people on

_____. Evenings

only. Need good English and

_____ skills.

Email Brenda at Brenda44@cup.org.

We need a great office

_____! Work

Monday through Friday, no

_____. Start

work _____ 9:00

_____ the morning.

3 How much are these?

1 Choose the correct sentences to complete this conversation.

☐ Oh, James. Thank you very much.   ☐ Well, I like it, but it's expensive.
☐ Which one?   ☑ Which ones?   ☐ Yes. But I don't really like yellow.

James: Look at those pants, Linda.

Linda: _Which ones?_

James: The yellow ones over there. They're nice.

Linda: _____

James: Hmm. Well, what about that sweater? It's perfect for you.

Linda: _____

James: This blue one.

Linda: _____

James: Hey, let me buy it for you. It's a present!

Linda: _____

2 Complete these conversations with *How much is/are . . . ?* and *this, that, these,* or *those.*

1. A: _How much is this_ blouse right here?

B: It's $47.95.

2. A: _____ glasses over there?

B: They're $87.

3. A: _____ sneakers right here?

B: They're $79.99.

4. A: _____ cat over there?

B: That's *my* cat, and he's not for sale!

3 Write the plurals of these words.

Spelling note: Plural nouns

Most words		Words ending in *-ss*, *-sh*, *-ch*, and *-x*	
cap	cap**s**	glass	glass**es**
shoe	sho**es**	dish	dish**es**
		watch	watch**es**

Words ending in *-f* and *-fe*		Words ending in consonant + *y*	
shelf	shel**ves**	country	countr**ies**
knife	kni**ves**		

1. ring ____rings____
2. glove _____
3. party _____
4. boy _____

5. tie _____
6. box _____
7. scarf _____
8. blouse _____

9. T-shirt _____
10. hairbrush _____
11. computer _____
12. dress _____

4 What do you think of these prices? Write a response.

That's cheap.   That's not bad.   That's reasonable.   That's pretty expensive!

1. $250 for a wool sweater
   That's pretty expensive!
2. $30 for a silk tie
   _____
3. $180 for a cotton dress
   _____

4. $40 for a gold necklace
   _____
5. $15 for three T-shirts
   _____
6. $80 for a leather belt
   _____

5 Choose the correct words to complete the conversations.

1. Shirley: I like ____those____ earrings over there.
       (that / those)

   Clerk: Which _____?
       (one / ones)

Shirley: The small gold _____.
       (one / ones)

   Clerk: _____ $399.
       (It's / They're)

Shirley: Oh, they're expensive!

2. George: Excuse me. How much
       are _____ pants?
       (that / those)

   Clerk: _____ only $65.
       (It's / They're)

George: And how much is _____ shirt?
       (this / these)

   Clerk: Which _____?
       (one / ones)

They're all different.

George: This green _____.
       (one / ones)

   Clerk: _____ $47.
       (It's / They're)

3.   **Clerk:** Good afternoon.

Martina: Oh, hi. How much is
       _____ watch?
       (this / these)

   Clerk: _____ $195.
       (It's / They're)

Martina: And how much is
       that _____?
       (one / ones)

   Clerk: _____ $99.
       (It's / They're)

Martina: That's not bad. I'll take it!

6 What do you make from these materials? Complete the chart using words from the box. (You will use words more than once.)

belt	boots	bracelet	button	gloves	hairbrush
jacket	necklace	pants	ring	shirt	

Cotton	Gold	Leather	Plastic	Silk	Wool
gloves					

7 Make comparisons using the words given. Add *than* if necessary.

1. A: Hey, look at these silver earrings! They're nice.
And they're _____ *cheaper than* _____ those gold earrings. (cheap)

B: But they're _____ the gold ones. (small)

A: Well, yeah. The gold ones are _____ the silver ones. (big) But $400 is a lot of money!

silver earrings

gold earrings

2. A: This leather coat is _____ the wool one. (attractive)

B: Yes, but the wool one is _____. (warm)

leather coat

wool coat

3. A: This orange shirt is an interesting color!

B: Yes, but the color is _____ the design. (pretty)

A: The design isn't bad.

B: I think the pattern on that gray shirt is _____ the pattern on this orange one. (good)

orange shirt

gray shirt

4. A: These cotton dresses are nice.

B: Yes, but the silk ones are _____. (nice)

A: They're also _____. (expensive)

cotton dresses

silk dresses

8 Complete the chart. Use the words from the box.

☑ boots   ☐ MP3 player   ☐ tablet
☐ bracelet   ☐ necklace   ☐ television
☐ dress   ☐ pants   ☐ T-shirt
☐ earrings   ☐ ring   ☐ smartphone

Clothing	Electronics	Jewelry
boots		

9 Answer these questions. Give your own information.

1 gold ring   2 tablet   3 hiking boots   4 wool gloves   5 black sunglasses

silver ring   laptop computer   sneakers   leather gloves   white sunglasses

1. Which ring do you prefer, the silver one or the gold one?
  I prefer the gold one.

2. Which one do you like more, the tablet or the laptop computer?

3. Which ones do you like more, the hiking boots or the sneakers?

4. Which ones do you prefer, the wool gloves or the leather gloves?

5. Which sunglasses do you like better, the black ones or the white ones?

10 Great gadgets!

A Read these ads. Match the pictures and descriptions.

1. _____   **2.** _____   **3.** _____   **4.** _____

a. Do you want to help the environment and do yard work at the same time? This machine knows when your lawn needs water. It waters your grass, and you don't have to do anything! Save time, save water, and save money! Only $124.99.

b. You can take this with you to the beach or on a picnic. No more uncomfortable towels or blankets! It fills with air in five minutes. Feel like you are sitting in your own living room in the great outdoors! Only $49.50.

c. What's a party without music? Indoors or outdoors, you can have a good time with this small item on a shelf or in a tree. Turn it down to set the mood, or turn it up to start the dancing! Only $299.99.

d. What's it like to swim like a fish? Now is your chance to find out! Put both feet in, get in the water, and feel what it's like to flap instead of kick. If you love to be in the water and dive deep, you need this! $36.

B Check (✓) True or False.

	True	False
1. The garden sensor waters your lawn when it needs more water.	☐	☐
2. The inflatable chair takes about five minutes to fill with air.	☐	☐
3. The Soundbook only works indoors.	☐	☐
4. You need two monofins, one for each foot.	☐	☐

C What's special about a gadget you have? Write a paragraph about it.

_____

_____

_____

_____

_____

_____

_____

4 Do you play the guitar?

1 Check (✓) the boxes to complete the survey about music and TV.

A Do you like these types of music?

	I love it!	It's OK.	I don't like it.
pop	☐	☐	☐
classical	☐	☐	☐
hip-hop	☐	☐	☐
rock	☐	☐	☐
jazz	☐	☐	☐

B Do you like these types of TV shows?

	I love them!	They're OK.	I don't like them.
talk shows	☐	☐	☐
reality shows	☐	☐	☐
sitcoms	☐	☐	☐
soap operas	☐	☐	☐
game shows	☐	☐	☐

2 What's your opinion? Answer the questions with the expressions and pronouns in the box.

	Object pronouns
Yes, I do.	
I love . . .	him
I like . . . a lot.	her
No, I don't.	it
I don't like . . . very much.	them
I can't stand . . .	

1. Do you like horror movies?
   Yes, I do. I like them a lot.

2. Do you like Kendrick Lamar?
   _____

3. Do you like heavy metal music?
   _____

4. Do you like mystery books?
   _____

5. Do you like video games?
   _____

6. Do you like Adele?
   _____

Kendrick Lamar

Adele

3 Choose the correct job for each picture.

☐ an actor ☐ an athlete ☐ a pop group ☐ a singer

1. Hope Solo is _____

2. Fall Out Boy are _____

3. Chris Hemsworth is

_____

_____

4. Luke Bryan is

_____

_____

4 Complete these conversations.

1. Ken: ___*Do*___ you ___*like*___ pop music, Janet?

   Janet: Yes, I _____ it a lot. I'm a big fan of Beyoncé.

   Ken: Oh, _____ she play the guitar?

   Janet: No, she _____, but she's a great dancer.

2. Alice: _____ kind of music _____ your

   parents _____, Jack?

   Jack: They _____ country music.

   Alice: Who _____ they _____?
   Jason Aldean?

   Jack: No, they _____ like him very much. They prefer Carrie Underwood.

3. Harold: Kelly, who's your favorite female singer? _____ you _____
   Selena Gomez?

   Kelly: No, I _____. I can't stand her. I like Etana.

   Harold: I don't know her. What kind of music _____ she sing?

   Kelly: She _____ reggae. She's really great!

5 Complete these questions and write answers.

1. <u>What kinds</u> of movies do you like?   <u>I like</u> _____
2. _____ is your favorite movie?   <u>My favorite</u> _____
3. _____ of movies do you dislike?   _____
4. _____ of TV shows do you like?   _____
5. _____ is your favorite actor or actress?   _____
6. _____ is your favorite song?   _____
7. _____ is your favorite rock band?   _____
8. _____ is your favorite video game?   _____

6 What do you think? Answer the questions.

1. Which are more interesting, action movies or historical dramas?

   _____

2. Which movies are more exciting, westerns or crime thrillers?

   _____

3. Which do you like more, musicals or animated movies?

   _____

4. Which do you prefer, romantic comedies or science fiction movies?

   _____

5. Which are scarier, horror movies or thrillers?

   _____

7 Verbs and nouns

A Which nouns often go with these verbs? Complete the chart. Use each noun only once.

listen to	play	watch
music		

☐ a basketball game   ☐ R&B
☐ the piano   ☐ the drums
☐ the guitar   ☑ music
☐ videos   ☐ a movie
☐ the radio

B Write a sentence using each verb in part A.

1. _____

2. _____

3. _____

8 Movie reviews

A Read the movie reviews. Write the type of movie for each review below the title.

comedy	historical drama	science fiction	crime thriller	horror
travel	documentary	romantic comedy	western	

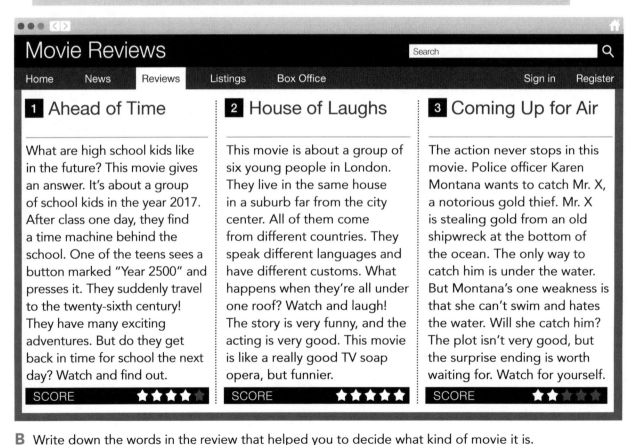

1 Ahead of Time

What are high school kids like in the future? This movie gives an answer. It's about a group of school kids in the year 2017. After class one day, they find a time machine behind the school. One of the teens sees a button marked "Year 2500" and presses it. They suddenly travel to the twenty-sixth century! They have many exciting adventures. But do they get back in time for school the next day? Watch and find out.

SCORE ★★★★☆

2 House of Laughs

This movie is about a group of six young people in London. They live in the same house in a suburb far from the city center. All of them come from different countries. They speak different languages and have different customs. What happens when they're all under one roof? Watch and laugh! The story is very funny, and the acting is very good. This movie is like a really good TV soap opera, but funnier.

SCORE ★★★★★

3 Coming Up for Air

The action never stops in this movie. Police officer Karen Montana wants to catch Mr. X, a notorious gold thief. Mr. X is stealing gold from an old shipwreck at the bottom of the ocean. The only way to catch him is under the water. But Montana's one weakness is that she can't swim and hates the water. Will she catch him? The plot isn't very good, but the surprise ending is worth waiting for. Watch for yourself.

SCORE ★★☆☆☆

B Write down the words in the review that helped you to decide what kind of movie it is.

1. Ahead of Time: <u>future,</u> _____

2. House of Laughs: _____

3. Coming Up for Air: _____

9 Choose the correct responses.

1. **A:** What do you think of "The Voice"?

   B: _I'm not a real fan of the show._
   - How about you?
   - I'm not a real fan of the show.

2. **A:** Do you like jazz music?

   B: _____
   - I can't stand it.
   - I can't stand them.

3. **A:** There's a soccer game tonight.

   B: _____
   - Thanks. I'd love to.
   - Great. Let's go.

4. **A:** Would you like to see a movie this weekend?

   B: _____
   - That sounds great!
   - I don't agree.

10 Yes or *no*?

A Fabiana is inviting friends to a movie. Do they accept the invitation or not? Check (✓) *Yes* or *No* for each response.

Accept?	Yes	No
1. I'd love to. What time does it start?	✓	☐
2. Thanks, but I don't really like animated movies.	☐	☐
3. That sounds great. Where is it?	☐	☐
4. I'd love to, but I have to work until midnight.	☐	☐
5. Thanks. I'd really like to. When do you want to meet?	☐	☐

B Respond to the invitations.

1. I have tickets to a classical concert on Saturday. Would you like to go?

   _____

2. There's a soccer game tonight. Do you want to go with me?

   _____

3. Meghan Trainor is performing tomorrow at the stadium. Would you like to see her?

   _____

11 Choose the correct phrases to complete these conversations.

1. Eva: _Do you like_____ pop music, Anita?
(Do you like / Would you like)

Anita: Yes, I do. _____ it a lot.
(I like / I'd like)

Eva: There's an Ariana Grande concert on Friday.
_____ to go with me?
(Do you like / Would you like)

Anita: Yes, _____! Thanks.
(I love to / I'd love to)

2. Marco: There's a baseball game on TV tonight.
_____ to come over and watch it?
(Do you like / Would you like)

Tony: _____, but I have to study tonight.
(I like to / I'd like to)

Marco: Well, _____ basketball?
(do you like / would you like)

Tony: Yes, _____. I love it!
(I do / I would)

Marco: There's a game on TV tomorrow at 3:00.
_____ to watch that with me?
(Do you like / Would you like)

Tony: _____. Thanks!
(I like to / I'd love to)

12 Rewrite these sentences. Find another way to say each sentence using the words given.

1. Do you like rap?
_What do you think of rap?_____ (think of)

2. Chad doesn't like country music.
_____ (can't stand)

3. I think soap operas are great!
_____ (love)

4. Celia doesn't like new age music.
_____ (be a fan of)

5. Do you want to go to a soccer match?
_____ (would like)

5 What an interesting family!

1 Which words are for males? Which are for females? Complete the chart.

- ☑ aunt
- ☑ brother
- ☐ daughter
- ☐ father
- ☐ husband
- ☐ mother
- ☐ nephew
- ☐ niece
- ☐ sister
- ☐ son
- ☐ uncle
- ☐ wife

Males			Females		
brother			aunt		

2 Complete this conversation. Use the present continuous of the verbs given.

Jan: You look tired, Monica.
_____Are you studying_____ (study) late at
night these days?

Monica: No, I'm not. My brother and sister
_____ (stay) with me
right now. They keep me up late every night.

Jan: Really, both of them? What
_____ (do) this
summer? _____ (take)
classes, too?

Monica: No, they aren't. My brother is on vacation
now, but he _____ (look)
for a part-time job here.

Jan: What about your sister?
_____ (work)?

Monica: Yes, she is. She has a part-time job at the university.
What about you, Jan? Are you in school this summer?

Jan: Yes, I am. I _____ (study) two languages.

Monica: Oh, _____ (take) Korean and Spanish again?

Jan: Well, I'm taking Korean, but now I _____ (start) Portuguese classes.

Monica: Really? That's exciting!

3 **What is another way to say each sentence? Rewrite the sentences using the words in the box.**

aunt	mother-in-law	~~uncle~~
granddaughter	son and daughter	~~wife~~

1. Anita is Marco's niece.

Marco is Anita's uncle.

2. John is married to Ann.

_____

3. My father's sister is a teacher.

_____

4. We have two children.

_____

5. My husband's mother is from Mexico.

_____

6. Willie and Mabel are Brooke's grandparents.

_____

4 **Choose the correct sentences to complete the conversation.**

- ☐ Yes, he is. He loves it there.
- ☑ No, I'm not. I'm living in Singapore now.
- ☐ Yes, we are. We really love Miami.
- ☐ Yes, I do. I like it a lot.
- ☐ No, they aren't. They're living in Atlanta now.

Kathy: Are you still living in Miami, Martin?

Martin: _No, I'm not. I'm living in Singapore now._

Kathy: Wow! Do you like it?

Martin: _____

Kathy: And is your brother still working in Seoul?

Martin: _____

Singapore

Kathy: And how about your parents? Are they still living in Florida?

Martin: _____ How about you and your family, Kathy? Are you still living here?

Kathy: _____

5 Complete these sentences. Use the simple present or the present continuous of the verbs given.

1. This is my cousin, Martin.

He _____lives_____ (live) in Houston, but

he _____ (visit) Peru this summer.

He _____ (take) cooking classes there.

2. And these are my parents.

They _____ (work) in Paris this year.

They _____ (be) on vacation right now.

3. Here's a photo of my grandparents.

They _____ (not work) now.

They _____ (be) retired.

4. This is my sister-in-law, Amanda.

She _____ (want) to start her
own company.

She _____ (study) business in
Australia right now.

5. And this is my nephew, George.

He _____ (go) to high school.

He _____ (like) history, but

he _____ (not like) chemistry.

6 Choose a friend or a family member. Write about him or her using the simple present and present continuous.

_____

_____

_____

_____

7 | Home or away?

A Answer these questions. Then read the passage.

1. Read the title below. What do you think a "boomerang kid" is?

_____

2. Are you going to live at home when you leave school? Why or why not?

_____

BOOMERANG KIDS _____

Today in the United States, many young adults are returning home to live after they graduate from college. They are being called "boomerang kids," like the Australian hunting stick that comes back after you throw it. Many college graduates can't find the jobs they want right away. Some also have college loans to pay back. They don't have enough money to rent expensive apartments, so they go back home to live with their parents. While they live at home, they are working at jobs with low pay and trying to save money for the future.

Meanwhile, the parents of boomerang kids are feeling the challenges of having their adult children back home. Most understand the problems their kids are having with money and accept that they're living with them again. But their relationships are different now. Some parents expect their kids to keep following their rules and to help around the house. Young adults, on the other hand, want to be independent and to make their own decisions. This creates tension between parents and kids. These boomerangs go out as kids, but they come back as adults.

B Check (✓) True or False. For statements that are false, write the correct information.

Young Adults	True	False
1. "Boomerang kids" are college graduates who don't want to live at home. _____	☐	☐
2. Many college graduates are having a difficult time finding a good job. _____	☐	☐
3. College graduates who live at home can't save money for the future. _____	☐	☐

Parents	True	False
4. Parents are seeing that it can be difficult to have their "boomerang kids" live at home again. _____	☐	☐
5. Parents want to do everything for their kids like they did when they were younger. _____	☐	☐
6. Parents and kids mostly agree about the rules and expectations of the house. _____	☐	☐

8 Arrange the quantifiers from the most to the least.

- ☑ all
- ☐ few
- ☐ many
- ☐ most
- ☐ nearly all
- ☑ no
- ☐ some

1. _____ all _____
2. _____
3. _____
4. _____
5. _____
6. _____
7. _____ no _____

9 Rewrite these sentences about the United States using the quantifiers given.

1. Ninety percent of children go to public schools. Ten percent of children go to private schools.

   Most _children go to public schools._
   Few _____
   _____

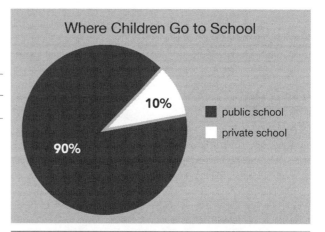

Where Children Go to School

10%
90%

■ public school
☐ private school

2. Sixty-two percent of young people go to college after they finish high school. Thirty-four percent of young people look for work.

   Many _____
   _____
   Some _____
   _____

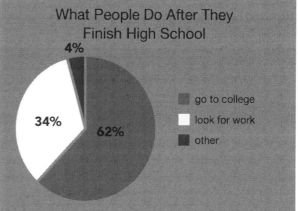

What People Do After They Finish High School

4%
34%
62%

■ go to college
☐ look for work
■ other

3. Ninety-five percent of people over 65 like to talk to family and friends. Forty-three percent of people over 65 like to spend time on a hobby. Three percent of people over 65 like to play soccer.

   Not many _____
   _____
   A lot of _____
   _____
   Nearly all _____

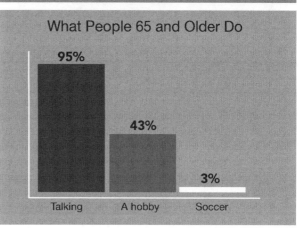

What People 65 and Older Do

95%
43%
3%
Talking   A hobby   Soccer

10 **Choose the correct words or phrases to complete this paragraph.**

In my country, some _____ couples _____ (couples / cousins / relatives) get married fairly young. Not many marriages _____ (break up / get divorced / stay together), and nearly all _____ (divorced / married / single) people remarry. Elderly couples often _____ (divorce again / move away / live at home) and take care of their grandchildren.

11 **Complete these sentences about your country. Use the words in the box.**

all	a lot of	few	most	nearly all	no	some

1. _____ young people go to college.

2. _____ people study English.

3. _____ married couples have more than five children.

4. _____ elderly people have part-time jobs.

5. _____ students have full-time jobs.

6. _____ children go to school on Saturdays.

6 How often do you run?

1 Complete the chart. Use words from the box.

baseball	soccer	basketball	volleyball	football
walking	jogging	weight training	Pilates	yoga

Sports	Fitness activities
baseball	

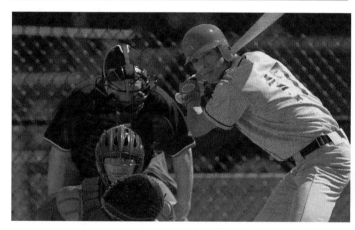

2 Arrange these words to make sentences or questions.

1. often   mornings   play   on   we   tennis   Saturday

   We often play tennis on Saturday mornings .

2. ever   Ryan   do   does   yoga

   _____?

3. go   do   often   swimming   how   you

   _____?

4. go   never   I   almost   jogging

   _____.

5. hardly   they   basketball   play   ever

   _____.

6. do   on   you   what   usually   Sundays   do

   _____?

3 Use these questions to complete the conversations: *How often do you . . . ?*
Do you ever . . . ? What do you usually . . . ?

1. **A:** *Do you ever go bowling?*

   B: Yes, I often go bowling on weekends.

2. **A:** _____

   B: Well, I usually do martial arts or watch TV after work.

3. **A:** _____

   B: Yes, I sometimes play sports on weekends – usually soccer.

4. **A:** _____

   B: I don't exercise very often at all.

5. **A:** _____

   B: No, I never go to the gym on Saturdays.

6. **A:** _____

   B: I usually go jogging four times a week.

4 **Keeping fit?**

A Check (✓) how often you do each of the things in the chart.

	Every day	Once or twice a week	Sometimes	Not very often	Never
do martial arts	☐	☐	☐	☐	☐
play basketball	☐	☐	☐	☐	☐
exercise	☐	☐	☐	☐	☐
go jogging	☐	☐	☐	☐	☐
go bowling	☐	☐	☐	☐	☐
play soccer	☐	☐	☐	☐	☐
go swimming	☐	☐	☐	☐	☐
do weight training	☐	☐	☐	☐	☐

B Write about your fitness habits using the information in the chart.

_____

_____

_____

_____

_____

_____

_____

5 Complete this conversation with the correct prepositions. Write them in the correct places.

Kelly: What time do you go swimming ^in the morning? (around / in / on)

Neil: I always go swimming 7:00. (at / for / on)

How about you, Kelly?

Kelly: I usually go swimming noon. (around / in / with)

I swim about 30 minutes. (at / for / until)

Neil: And do you also play sports your free time? (at / in / until)

Kelly: No, I usually go out my classmates. (around / for / with)

What about you?

Neil: I go to the gym Mondays and Wednesdays. (at / on / until)

And sometimes I go jogging weekends. (for / in / on)

Kelly: Wow! You really like to stay in shape.

6 Complete the sentences. Use the words from the box.

| do | ice hockey | soccer | treadmill | goes | jogging |
| swimming | watches | exercises | shape | training | |

1. Katie never ___exercises___ .
   She's a real couch potato.

2. How often do you _____ martial arts?

3. I like to stay in _____. I play sports every day.

4. Jeff does weight _____ every evening. He lifts 50-pound weights.

5. Arturo goes _____ twice a week. He usually runs about three miles.

6. Miho often _____ TV in the evening.

7. Maria is on the _____ team at her high school. She's good at passing the ball.

8. Judy never goes _____ when the water is cold.

9. Kyle often _____ bike riding on weekends.

10. I run on the _____ at the gym three times a week.

11. In Canada, many people like to play _____ outside in the winter.

7 Sports around the world

A Read the descriptions of three unique sports that are played in different parts of the world. Which sport do you want to try? Why?

Capoeira

Capoeira is a sport that comes from Brazil. It is part martial art, part dance, and part game. The legs do most of the work in this sport. Capoeiristas kick, jump, and dance to the music of stringed instruments, drums, bells, and rattles. Although the two people are fighting and defending themselves, capoeira is really more about movement, speed, and knowing what your opponent is thinking.

Hurling

The game of hurling comes from Ireland. It is the fastest field sport in the world. Hurlers play on a field like soccer but use a stick and a small ball. The stick is used to carry or hit the ball, or players can kick it or slap it with their hands. They try to get the ball over a bar for one point or under the bar into a net for three points. Hurling is a very old sport and similar to modern rugby, soccer, field hockey, and football.

Bashi

Bashi is a national sport in the Maldives, and only women play it. Between eight and eleven women play on a tennis court with tennis balls and one tennis racket. One player hits a ball with the racket on one side of the net, and players try to catch it on the other side. The woman who hits the ball faces away from the net and has to hit the ball backwards over her head! Women often get injured trying to catch the fast-moving balls with their bare hands.

B What sport do the activities describe? Check (✓) the answers.

	Capoeira	Hurling	Bashi
1. hit a ball backwards	☐	☐	☐
2. run very fast	☐	☐	☐
3. know what your opponent is thinking	☐	☐	☐
4. get a ball in a net	☐	☐	☐
5. move with music	☐	☐	☐
6. hit a ball over a net	☐	☐	☐

8 Choose the correct responses.

1. A: How often do you play golf, Monica?

    B: *Once a week.*

- I guess I'm OK.
- Once a week.
- About an hour.

2. A: How long do you spend on the golf course?

    B: _____

- About four hours.
- About average.
- About three miles.

3. A: And how well do you play?

    B: _____

- I'm not very well.
- I almost never do.
- I'm about average.

4. A: How good are you at other sports?

    B: _____

- Not very good, actually.
- I sometimes play twice a week.
- Pretty well, I guess.

9 Look at the answers. Write questions using *how*.

1. A: *How long do you spend exercising?* _____

    B: I don't spend any time at all. In fact, I don't exercise.

2. A: _____ at playing football?

    B: I'm pretty good at it. I'm on the school team.

3. A: _____ for a walk?

    B: Almost every day. I really enjoy it.

4. A: _____

    B: Baseball? Pretty well, I guess. Yeah, I like it a lot.

5. A: _____

    B: I spend about an hour jogging.

10 Rewrite these sentences. Find another way to say each sentence using the words given.

1. I don't go bike riding very often.

    I hardly ever go bike riding.   (hardly ever)

2. Tamara exercises twice a month.

    _____   (not very often)

3. Patty tries to keep fit.

    _____   (stay in shape)

4. Ricardo often exercises at the gym.

    _____   (work out)

5. I go jogging every day after work.

    _____   (always)

6. How good are you at tennis?

    _____   (play)

11 What do you think about fitness and sports? Answer these questions.

1. Do you like to exercise for a short time or a long time?

    _____

    _____

2. Do you prefer exercising in the morning or in the evening?

    _____

    _____

3. Which do you like better, walking or jogging?

    _____

    _____

4. Which do you like better, team sports or individual sports?

    _____

    _____

5. How good are you at sports like basketball and tennis?

    _____

    _____

6. What is a sport or game you don't like?

    _____

    _____

7 We went dancing!

1 Past tense

A Write the simple past of these regular verbs.

1. watch   _watched_   **4.** arrive _____ **7.** travel _____
2. play _____   **5.** study _____ **8.** wash _____
3. invite _____   **6.** hurry _____ **9.** look _____

B Write the simple present form of these irregular simple past verbs.

1. _____eat_____ ate   **5.** _____ slept
2. _____ did   **6.** _____ spent
3. _____ met   **7.** _____ drove
4. _____ saw   **8.** _____ went

C Use two of the verbs above and write sentences about the past.

Example: _We saw the Eiffel Tower in Paris last year._

1. _____

2. _____

2 Use the cues to answer these questions.

1. Where did you go this weekend?

  I went to the zoo. _____ (to the zoo)

2. Who did you meet at the party?

  _____ (a famous artist)

3. What did you buy?

  _____ (a new pair of jeans)

4. How did you and Mario like the movie?

  _____ (a lot)

5. Where did Faye and Bob spend their vacation?

  _____ (in the country)

6. What time did you and Allison get home?

  _____ (a little after 1:00)

3 What do you like to do alone? With other people? Complete the chart with activities from the box. Then add one more activity to each list.

cook dinner
do homework
exercise
go shopping
go to a sports event
go to the movies
have a picnic
play video games
take a vacation
watch TV

Activities I like to do alone	Activities I like to do with other people

4 Complete the questions in this conversation.

A: How _did you spend the weekend_ ?

B: I spent the weekend with my sisters.

A: What _____?

B: Well, on Saturday, we went shopping.

A: That sounds like fun! What _____?

B: I bought a new pair of shoes and a new purse.

A: Where _____ on Sunday?

B: We went to an amusement park.

A: Oh, how _____?

B: We had a great time. In fact, we stayed there all day.

A: Really? What time _____?

B: We got home very late, around midnight.

5 **Answer these questions with negative statements. Then add a positive statement using the information in the box.**

☐ finish the project on Saturday   ☐ take the bus
☐ go out with friends   ☐ watch it on TV
☑ stay home all weekend   ☐ work all day until six o'clock

1. A: Did you and John go to Anne's party on Saturday?

   B: _No, we didn't. We stayed home all weekend._

2. A: Beth left work at 2:00 yesterday afternoon. Did you go home early, too?

   B: _____

3. A: I watched TV all weekend. Did you spend the weekend at home, too?

   B: _____

4. A: I saw you and Amy at the library on Saturday. Did you work together on Sunday, too?

   B: _____

5. A: Giovanni drove me to work yesterday morning. Did you drive to work?

   B: _____

6. A: Sandy went to the baseball game last night. Did you and Martin go to the game?

   B: _____

6 **Read about Pamela's week. Match the sentences that have a similar meaning.**

A	B
1. She was broke last week. _f_	**a.** She had people over.
2. She didn't work on Monday. _____	**b.** She did housework.
3. She worked around the house. _____	**c.** She took the day off.
4. She didn't wash the clothes. _____	**d.** She had a good time.
5. She invited friends for dinner. _____	**e.** She didn't do the laundry.
6. She had a lot of fun. _____	✓ **f.** She spent all her money.

7 Did we take the same trip?

A Read the posts. Who went to Bangkok for the first time?

JOSEPH

We went to Thailand again for our summer vacation. We spent a week in Bangkok and did something every day. We went to the floating market very early one morning. We didn't buy anything there – we just looked. Another day, we went to Wat Phra Kaew, the famous Temple of the Emerald Buddha. Check out my pic!

Then we saw two more temples nearby. We also went on a river trip somewhere outside Bangkok. The best thing about the trip was the food. The next time we have friends over for dinner, I'm going to cook Thai food.

OLIVIA

Last summer, we spent our vacation in Thailand. We were very excited – it was our first trip there. We spent two days in Bangkok. Of course, we got a river taxi to the floating market. We bought some delicious fruit there. I'm posting a picture.

The next day we went to a very interesting temple called the Temple of the Emerald Buddha. We didn't have time to visit any other temples. However, we went to two historic cities – Ayutthaya and Sukhothai. Both have really interesting ruins. Everything was great. It's impossible to say what the best thing was about the trip.

B Who did these things on their trip? Check (✓) all correct answers.

	Joseph	Olivia
1. stayed for two days in Bangkok	☐	✓
2. visited the floating market	☐	☐
3. bought fruit	☐	☐
4. saw some historic ruins	☐	☐
5. traveled on the river	☐	☐
6. loved the food the most	☐	☐
7. enjoyed everything	☐	☐

8 Complete this conversation with *was, wasn't, were,* or *weren't.*

A: How _____was_____ your vacation in Thailand, Rich?

B: It _____ great. I really enjoyed it.

A: How long _____ you there?

B: We _____ there for two weeks.

A: _____ you in Bangkok the whole time?

B: No, we _____. We _____ in the mountains for a few days.

A: And how _____ the weather? _____ it good?

B: No, it _____ good at all! In fact, it _____ terrible. The city _____ very hot, and the mountains _____ cold and rainy!

9 Choose the correct questions to complete this conversation.

☐ And what was the best part?
☐ How long were you in Brazil?
☑ How was your vacation in South America?
☐ And how long were you in Argentina?
☐ How was the weather?

A: _How was your vacation in South America?_

B: It was a great trip. I really enjoyed Brazil and Argentina.

A: _____

B: I was in Brazil for ten days.

A: _____

B: For about eight days.

A: Wow, that's a long time! _____

B: It was hot and sunny the whole time.

A: _____

B: It was definitely the beaches in Brazil. Oh, and we learned the tango in Argentina!

Brazil

10 Complete the sentences with the correct words or phrases. Use the past tense when necessary.

1. We _____ a trip to Egypt last summer. (take / make / do)

2. My brothers _____ at home all weekend. (go dancing / play video games / take a bike ride)

3. I worked really hard in Germany last week. I was there _____. (in my car / on business / on vacation)

4. I'm sorry I was late. I had to _____ a phone call. (do / make / go)

5. I stayed home last night and _____ the laundry. (do / go / make)

11 My kind of vacation

A What do you like to do on vacation? Rank these activities from 1 (you like it the most) to 6 (you like it the least).

_____ go to the beach

_____ visit historical places

_____ go shopping

_____ visit museums

_____ spend time at home

_____ eat good food

B Answer these questions about vacations.

1. How often do you go on vacation?

_____

2. How much time do you spend on vacation?

_____

3. Who do you usually go with?

_____

4. Where do you like to go?

_____

5. What do you usually do on vacation?

_____

8 How's the neighborhood?

1 Places

A Match the words in columns A and B. Write the names of the places.

A	B		
☑ coffee	☐ campus	**1.**	*coffee shop*
☐ college	☑ shop	**2.**	
☐ gas	☐ hotspot	**3.**	
☐ grocery	☐ office	**4.**	
☐ hair	☐ mall	**5.**	
☐ movie	☐ salon	**6.**	
☐ post	☐ station	**7.**	
☐ shopping	☐ store	**8.**	
☐ Wi-Fi	☐ theater	**9.**	

B Write questions with *Is there a . . . ?* or *Are there any . . . ?* and the names of places from part A.

1. A: I need a haircut. _Is there a hair salon_____ near here?

    B: Yes, there's one on Grand Street.

2. A: I want to buy some new clothes. _____ near here?

    B: No, there isn't, but there's one in Center City.

3. A: I need to mail this package. _____ around here?

    B: Yes, there's one next to the bank.

4. A: I want to see a movie tonight. _____ around here?

    B: Yes, there's one in the shopping mall.

5. A: We need some gas. _____ on this street?

    B: No, there aren't, but there are a couple on Second Avenue.

6. A: We need to buy some cereal and some apples.

    _____ near here?

    B: Yes, there's one near the gym on Brown Street.

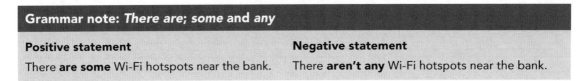

2 **Look at these street maps of Springfield and Riverside. There are ten differences between them. Find the other eight.**

Grammar note: *There are; some and any*

Positive statement	**Negative statement**
There **are some** Wi-Fi hotspots near the bank.	There **aren't any** Wi-Fi hotspots near the bank.

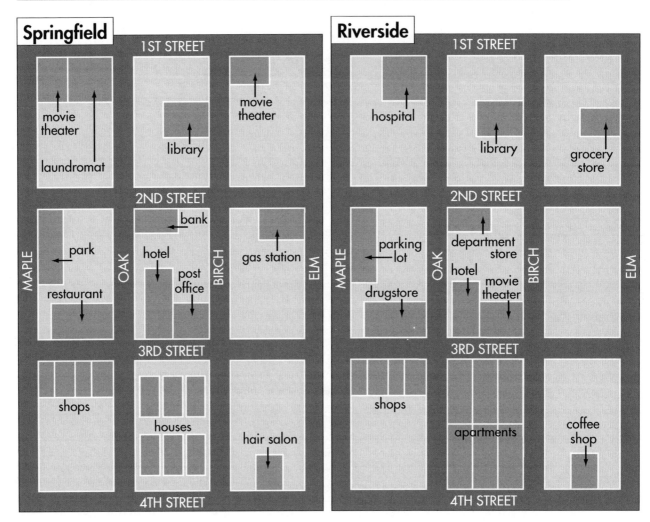

1. There are some movie theaters on 1st Street in Springfield, but there aren't any in Riverside.
2. There's a park on the corner of 2nd Street and Maple in Springfield, but there isn't one in Riverside. There's a parking lot.
3. _____
4. _____
5. _____
6. _____
7. _____
8. _____
9. _____
10. _____

3 Answer these questions. Use the map and the prepositions in the box.

☐ across from   ☐ between   ☐ in
☐ near   ☑ next to   ☐ on the corner of

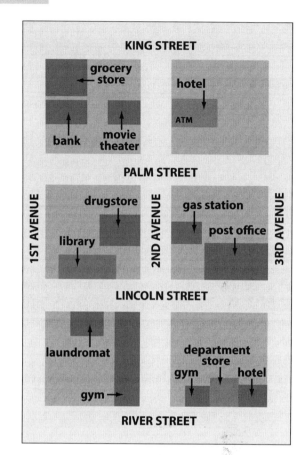

1. Where's the nearest bank?
   There's one next to the grocery store
   on 1st Avenue.

2. Is there a post office near here?
   Yes. There
   _____

3. I'm looking for a drugstore.
   _____
   _____

4. Is there a laundromat in this neighborhood?
   _____
   _____

5. Is there a department store on River Street?
   _____
   _____

6. Are there any ATMs around here?
   _____
   _____

4 Answer these questions about your city or neighborhood. Use the expressions in the box and your own information.

Yes, there is. There's one on . . .   Yes, there are. There are some on . . .
No, there isn't.   No, there aren't.

1. Are there any good coffee shops around the school? _____
   _____

2. Is there a drugstore near the school? _____
   _____

3. Are there any grocery stores in your neighborhood? _____
   _____

4. Is there a laundromat close to your home? _____
   _____

A Read the interviews. Where would Charles like to live? Where would Arlene like to live?

M O D E R N
L I V I N G

HOME | STORIES | PHOTOS

WE ASKED TWO PEOPLE ABOUT THE PLACES THEY LIVE.

Charles Bell

"My neighborhood is very convenient — it's near the shopping center and the bus station. It's also safe. But those are the only good things about living downtown. It's very noisy because the streets are always full of people! The traffic is terrible, and parking is a big problem! I can never park on my own street. I'd like to live in a small town."

Arlene Miller

"My family and I live in a nice small town. It has a great square where people meet for social events, and there's music on summer evenings. It's a safe place to raise children. But there is no privacy here. Everyone in town knows what you are doing all the time. And I don't meet as many interesting people as when I lived in the city. It can be too quiet here. I want more action! I think it's better downtown."

♡ LIKE   COMMENT

B How do Charles and Arlene feel about their neighborhoods? Complete the chart.

	Advantages	Disadvantages
Downtown	convenient	
Small Town		no privacy

C Do you think it's better to live downtown or in a small town? Why?

_____

_____

_____

D How do you feel about the place you live? Write about it.

_____

_____

_____

6 Complete the chart. Use words from the box.

☑ bank   ☐ library   ☐ people   ☐ theater
☑ crime   ☐ noise   ☐ pollution   ☐ traffic
☐ hospital   ☐ parking   ☐ school   ☐ water

Count nouns		Noncount nouns	
bank		crime	

7 Write questions using *How much . . . ?* or *How many . . . ?* Then look at the picture and write answers to the questions. Use the expressions in the box.

☐ a few   ☐ a lot   ☐ many
☐ none   ☐ not any   ☑ only a little

1. trash   How much trash is there?   There's only a little.
2. buses   _____   _____
3. traffic   _____   _____
4. bicycles   _____   _____
5. police officers   _____   _____
6. crime   _____   _____

8 Choose the correct words or phrases to complete the conversation.

Andrea: Are there _____any_____ (any / one / none) coffee shops around here, Carlos?

Carlos: Sure. There are _____ (any / one / a lot). There's a coffee shop _____ (across from / between / on) the Daily Market, but it's expensive.

Andrea: Well, are there _____ (any / none / one) others?

Carlos: Yeah, there are _____ (a few / a little / one). There's a nice _____ (any / one / some) near here. It's called Morning Joe.

Andrea: That's perfect! Where is it, exactly?

Carlos: It's on Third Avenue, _____ (between / on / on the corner of) the National Bank and the Chinese restaurant.

Andrea: So let's go!

9 Choose the correct words or phrases.

1. I'm going to the grocery store to get some _____.
    (clothes / gas / food)

2. We're taking a long drive. We need to stop at the _____.
    (laundromat / gas station / drugstore)

3. I live on the 8th floor of my _____.
    (apartment building / neighborhood / theater)

4. Our apartment is in the center of the city. We live _____.
    (downtown / in the neighborhood / in the suburbs)